Kylie Minogue

Mike Wilson

Published in association with The Basic Skills Agency

Hodder & Stoughton

A MEMBER OF THE HODDER HEADLINE GROUP

Acknowledgements
Cover: Sipa Press/REX FEATURES

Photos: p. 2 © Niviere/DPPI – SIPA/Rex Features; p. 7 © Rex Features; p. 9 © PA Photos;
p. 13 © Andrew Murray/Rex Features; p. 16 © Austral International/Rex Features; p. 22
© Sipa Press/Rex Features; P. 25 © Brian Rasic/Rex Features.

Orders; please contact Bookpoint Ltd, 130 Milton Park, Abingdon, Oxon OX14 4SB.
Telephone (44) 01235 827720, Fax: (44) 01235 400454. Lines are open from 9.00–6.00,
Monday to Saturday, with a 24 hour message answering service.
You can also order through our website www.hodderheadline.co.uk

British Library Cataloguing in Publication Data
A catalogue record for this title is available from the British Library

ISBN 0 340 87648 4

First published 2003
Impression number   10 9 8 7 6 5 4 3 2 1
Year   2007 2006 2005 2004 2003

Copyright © Mike Wilson 2003

Typeset by SX Composing DTP, Rayleigh, Essex.
Printed in Great Britain for Hodder & Stoughton Educational, a division of Hodder
Headline, 338 Euston Road, London NW1 3BH by Bath Press Ltd, Bath.

Contents

1 Kylie

'When I was little,' says Kylie,
'I was just like every other little girl.
I was pretty normal, pretty shy.

'I used to hang out with my friends.
We'd play at being pop stars.
We'd sing Abba songs
into a hairbrush
up in my room.

'I always knew I wanted to be a singer.
I wanted to be Olivia Newton-John
or Madonna.'

Today, Kylie Minogue is a big star,
as big as Madonna.
And Madonna gives her respect.

What is the secret of her success?

How did a shy little girl
from Melbourne, Australia
get to take on the world –
and win?

Kylie at the closing ceremony of the 2000 Olympic Games.

2 Sibling Rivalry

Kylie Minogue was born
in Melbourne, Australia
on 28 May 1968.

Kylie is an Australian word.
It means 'boomerang'!

Show-business was in the family.

Kylie's mum, Carol, had been a ballet dancer.
Her aunt was an actress.
Then there was Dannii.

Danii was Kylie's little sister.
Kylie was the quiet and shy one,
Dannii was the show-off.
Kylie was keen on sewing.
Dannii was always singing and dancing.

It was Dannii who first got a job in TV.
She was just seven years old.

Dannii had an audition
to act in a top TV soap.
Their mum took Kylie along too.

Kylie got the job.

Dannii was upset.
Then she got some TV work too.
Soon, Dannii was a famous child-star.
Kylie was in the shade.

By the time Dannii was 11,
she had a job on a TV show
called 'Young Talent Time'.

Kylie's job was to help her sister
respond to all her fan mail.

It can't have been easy.

'We got on pretty well,' Kylie said later.
'But I did get a bit fed up.
I was just "Dannii's big sister".
Dannii was the famous one.'

3 Neighbours

In January 1986,
Kylie got the job that changed her life.

Neighbours was a clean-cut TV soap
about life in sunny Australia.

But the show was not doing so well.
It needed new story-lines.
It needed new, younger actors.

Kylie got the part of Charlene.
Charlene was a pretty young girl.
She wanted to work with cars.

Charlene was a bit of a rebel –
sometimes a bit headstrong.

She was gutsy too.
She had plenty of common sense.

She went down well
with the show's teenage viewers.
Soon *Neighbours* was a huge hit
all over the world.

Kylie's 12-week contract was torn up.
She had a job for life!

Kylie as Charlene in 1988.

4 Jason

Kylie met Jason Donovan on a TV show.
They were both 11 years old.
(Kylie is four days older than Jason.)
Back then, Jason was just a chubby little kid.

Then Jason joined the cast of *Neighbours*.
So did Kylie.
They were both 17.
Jason wasn't chubby any more – he was cute.

Jason played Scott, Kylie's boyfriend.
In her very first scene,
Kylie had to punch Jason.
It was clear that love was in the air.

In fact,
Scott and Charlene got married
in July 1987.
20 million people tuned in
to watch the wedding.

Kylie with Jason Donovan.

Charlene and Scott were a couple
on the screen.
Kylie and Jason were a couple
off the screen.

They said they were just good friends.

It would be bad for the show
if people knew about them.

It was their secret.

For Kylie,
Jason was her first love.
She kept the secret
for nearly four years.

Kylie left *Neighbours* in June 1988.
Jason left a year later.

Kylie's singing career was taking off.
'The Loco-Motion' was a hit in 1987.
'I Should Be So Lucky' followed in 1988.

Jason had a few hit singles too.
They even had a hit together –
'Especially For You'.

But Kylie and Jason were growing apart.
They were working hard on their careers.
They were apart a lot.

In the end it was all too much.
Kylie ended it with Jason.

Jason had been so cute and clean-cut.
So boy-next-door,
So *Neighbours* . . .

Who would Kylie turn to next?

5 Excess

Jason took Kylie to see INXS.
She met the singer
Michael Hutchence.

Michael was drunk.
He asked Kylie to go to bed with him.
(Kylie said no.
She was still with Jason at the time.)

A year later,
Michael met Kylie again.
They started dating.

Kylie with Michael Hutchence.

Michael and Kylie made an odd couple.
She was a soap star.
She had a string of pop hits.

He was a crazy rock star.
He was into sex and drugs.
He was into rock-and-roll.

What did they see in each other?

Kylie was just 21.
She still lived with her mum and dad.
She liked sewing.

Michael was sexy and dangerous.
He lived life on the edge.

'After our first date,' Kylie says,
'everyone went back to his hotel room.
I saw things I'd never seen before.'

It was true love.

Kylie said,

'People think Michael is just wild.

It's not true. He's so deep and intense.

He's smart, and well-read.

He loved me – no questions asked.'

Michael said,

'I love Kylie.

I'm so proud of her.

I love teaching her.

I love watching her grow.

And I learn from her . . .'

It didn't last.

After 18 months,

Michael ended it.

He was seeing other women.

Women like actress Patsy Kensit.

Women like supermodel Helena Christensen.

'I was so hurt,' Kylie said.

'I was so in love with him.

I spent a long time crying my heart out.'

In 1997, Michael's rock-and-roll lifestyle
came to an end.
He was found dead in a hotel room.
No one knows if he wanted to kill himself,
but it was clear
that sex and drugs had played a part.

Kylie was strong for the funeral.
'I still miss him,' she said.
'But I know he's looking down, now, laughing.
I know he's still teaching me.'

Kylie at Michael's funeral.

6 Sexy

After the split with Michael,
Kylie lost herself in her work.

She changed record labels.
She moved away from bubbly pop songs.
She became a serious dance artist.
Her hits were played in all the top clubs.

Kylie also tried working
with a lot of other music stars.
She worked with Prince, Nick Cave, Deee-lite
and the Manic Street Preachers.

And Kylie had a new love.
A fashion photographer named Stephane.

Kylie changed her image.
She wasn't cute and cuddly any more.
Now she was sexy.

By 1997,
Kylie had a new CD.
It was going to be called *Impossible Princess*.
That was how Kylie saw herself.
But then Princess Diana died
The name of the album had to be changed.
Now Kylie had two albums,
one after the other,
both called *Kylie Minogue*!

But Kylie was not happy.
She'd split up with Stephane.
Her new, rocky dance singles were not selling well.
Her record company went bust.
Kylie spent New Year's Eve
crying her eyes out.

It took until June 2000.
Then Kylie bounced back,
bigger and better than ever!

Her first new single was 'Spinning Around'.
It was perfect pop.
It was what Kylie did best!

In the video,
Kylie wore gold hot pants.
She'd got them for 50 pence
from a market years before.

Kylie says
'It was the best 50p I ever spent!'

Britain fell in love with Kylie again!
And with her bottom!
The Sun said Kylie's bum was a national treasure.
One magazine liked Kylie's bottom so much
they gave her an award for 'Services to Mankind'!

More massive hits followed.
'Can't Get You Out Of My Head'
was another perfect pop song.
It won an award – 'Best Dance Song'.
It went straight to number one
and was the bestselling single of the year.

7 James

'You work and work and work,' says Kylie.
'And then you go – Oh, I'm 33.
Am I going to have children?
I'd better think about that.'

Kylie met James Gooding in 2000.
He was a model.
He had been in some TV adverts.
He was 28, five years younger.
He'd fancied Kylie since he was 14!

They were at the Brit Awards together,
in 2000.
The rumours started.
Was Kylie thinking of settling down?

'I have settled down,' she says. 'Three times.
But it doesn't last, for some reason.
I love James,' she goes on.
'This one really could be Mr. Right.'

Kylie with James Gooding in 2002.

8 Breaking Up Is Hard To Do

They lasted two years.
In August 2002,
Kylie and James split up.

Kylie blamed her work.
'I'm used to this life,
but it's unfair on James.
We are going to stay friends . . .'

Things hadn't been right for some time.
Kylie got angry
when James flirted with other women.
The media pressure got to them.
'Sometimes it's hard being Kylie,' she said.

James said 'Kylie will always be special to me.'

They have been seen together.
Will they get back together?

Kylie was seen with
French heart-throb
Oliver Martinez in March 2003.

As one ex has said,
'Kylie likes her freedom.
She's a very free spirit.
I don't think she's ever
going to belong to anybody.'

9 The Princess of Pop

'I'm normal, I guess,' says Kylie.
'I look all right. I sing all right.
I can dance a bit.'

Kylie brings beauty and glamour
and fun to all the things she does.

And she does so many different things.

She spoke the words
of 'I Should Be So Lucky'
at a poetry reading
at the Royal Albert Hall.

She sang at the close
of the Sydney Olympics in October 2000.

She acted in a Shakespeare play.
She was in the crazy cult-movie *Moulin Rouge*.

She sang 'Kids' with Robbie Williams
at the MTV Music Awards in November 2000.

Kylie singing with Robbie Williams.

She sang 'Sisters Are Doing It For Themselves'
with Elton John – for all her gay fans.

She modelled for Oxfam.
she modelled sexy clothes for *Agent Provocateur*.
She designs the *Love Kylie* range.

For one song she dressed up as Marilyn Monroe.
For another song she dressed as Madonna.

'Madonna is the Queen of Pop,' Kylie has said.
'And I am the Princess.'

At the MTV Music Awards in 2000,
Madonna gave Kylie respect.
Madonna wore a t-shirt
with 'Kylie Minogue' on the front.

Then in July 2002,
Madonna wrote a song for Kylie.
It was called 'Alone Again'.
The Queen of Pop
has never given a song away before.

Kylie knew it was an honour.

10 Where Next?

'For a long time,' Kylie says,
'my career has come first.

My personal life has had to come second,
and that's not so good.'

Will Kylie put love before her career now?
If she wants to start a family,
now's the time.
But will she ever find a man
to settle down with?

Or will Kylie always be
the restless, hard-working
Princess of Pop?